T0129269

INVISIBLE PRINCE

Invisible Prince

Frances Mahan

INVISIBLE PRINCE

iUniverse books may be ordered through booksellers or by contacting:

iUniverse
1663 Liberty Drive
Bloomington, IN 47403
www.iuniverse.com
1-800-Authors (1-800-288-4677)

ISBN: 978-1-5320-1100-9 (sc)
ISBN: 978-1-5320-1099-6 (e)

Library of Congress Control Number: 2016919740

Print information available on the last page.

iUniverse rev. date: 03/21/2017

THE PROLOGUE

In a far Arab region of the Middle East, two men are unaware of the love an older woman has for them. This woman's love transforms the lives of both men with powerful colloquial words, and communication of the mind at a distance. The two men are good friends. However, they have never met this woman before. Thus, by the virtue and the nature of her mind, they become rivals. One day, the woman crosses path with the Indian actor without knowing of his presence in India. The encounter happen before she began her communication at a distance with them.

In this scene, she is a spirit of the past in love with an entangle web of imagination of her lost love of her children. In her mind, she loves both equally. One is her soul mate, the other, has stolen her heart forever.

She is tormented by this unfamiliar way of loving. In the process, she loses her mind and death cometh and goes inside her soul as she dies and relives to love them again and again. During her journey, she loves them and hates them at the same time. This love triangle goes on for three years with many tears and suffering. Her vision of love for these two men comes from the lack of connection she misses with her three dead children. Thus, in an effort to forget about these men, she begins a spooky communication at a distance with a third man in the US, where the story will end.

In Dubai where this story takes place, a twelve year old relationship has been broken. The saga of a woman and her three lovers at a distance had just begun. She is certain that from a quantum level, she communicates with all three of them at an emotional, visual and mental level. She feels their presence before her and knows what they are doing in the present time. She tunes in this network through a medium of meditation. She dances to connect to her spirit and tune in to their minds. Her abilities are unlike any other human being. She communicates at a distance through emails and messages to unknown people she have picked randomly. In the next hour, we will watch the entire scenes of how she daydreams and talks to her three lovers with her mindset.

ACT 1 SCENE 1

ELIZABETH

Who are thou my prince, I ask myself? Are thou
simply an illusion of my own making or a passion
of my heart. I dream of thee like a dreamer lost
in a dream of an unknown world. My thoughts of
thee bring my mind to connect with thy senses. My
thoughts of thee are as real as each breath I here take.
Who are thou, my prince, whose image cometh to me
and go like an angel or devil? Who are thou?

THE PRINCE

Who are thou old woman whose anxious
impertinence cometh to me without announcing thy
presence. Move on old rag!

ELIZABETH

I am a reality that cometh to thee in a vision like a
ghost. In my dreams, thou are a revelation of love.
Thou are the presence of innocence in a child, an
angle and beast at the same time.

THE PRINCE

This peasant woman, removed her at once!

ELIZABETH

I have felt thy heart in mine from the moment I set
my eyes on thee for the first time. Thou noticed
me not, my presence see thee at glance like a thief
in the night. Why my dear prince, why? Are thou
a revelation of a story that began with a dream. A
simple revelation of a prince I do not know. One who
is invisible to my eyes, yet I sense and feel with my
mind deep within the core of my heart. Why doth thee
sees me as evil when purity thou possess not even in
thy blood.

THE PRINCE

Why cometh to me? I care not for thy love thy
presence nor thy existence. What has prompted thy
ego to seek for me? Why, who are thou woman, whose
presence nor old profile appeals not to me.

ELIZABETH

I have seeing thee as a boy with the strength of thy
father holding thee with captivating protection in his
arms. I saw him in a dream of mine. It was a message
from the highest power of the universe.

THE PRINCE

Tell me not of thy stupid mental illusions. For I care
the list about thy foolish dream, feelings or stories.
Get out! At once! Get out! "Old stupid woman"; who

allowed this creature in my palace of peace? Allah! Guard!

GUARD

Yes my prince. At your service!

THE PRINCE

Get this old woman out of my palace at once. Now! Allow not one to enter my private confines without my authority. Understood?

GUARD

Yes, your majesty, my Prince. I will, immediately.

ELIZABETH

He was always in my mind, in my heart, but now, I despise him. To believe that I, this foolish old woman could have fallen for such an aristocrat thinking that maybe, just maybe, he was a kind and considered prince. How foolish of me. A prince, what is a prince anyways. He is but an Arab prince of intolerable arrogance. He is a prince covered with a veil and crown of an angel with more secrets than jewels. He came into my life like a thief in the night to steal my heart. That's who thou are. A thief of hearts. I hate thee, Prince of hearts. Thou are but a bundle of ego without sentiment nor faith. Who are thou prince of hearts who touches me with thy hands and sends me down into the pitfalls of hell! Where I feel death cometh upon me. Who are thou! Are thou a man, a ghost or simply God showing me love in a mystical way? Who are thou my prince of hearts.

THE PRINCE

Father, I never invited the old rag into our premises. She most had trespassed while the guards were busy. I have no idea who the devil she is.

FATHER

Allowed me to extend my advice for once my son; never underestimate the wisdom of an older woman. I know, I know, thou are young, vibrant and full of life. Perhaps she has cometh to teach thee something of merit.

THE PRINCE

O father, thy old school teaches thee nothing like our time. The old can never replace the new.

FATHER

One day my dear prince, Words of wisdom will be of thee to share.

BROTHER

Are we on? The car race and the ladies is all tonight! And tomorrow, we will be jumping from the skies again. Come brother, let's go! The ladies are waiting.

THE PRINCE

I have to go. My competition begins at five in the morning. This is an early star for me brother. Enjoy the party.

BROTHER

Thou are turning into an old man. O I see, it must be the old lady I heard about.

THE PRINCE

I will not tolerate such comments of me and that old woman. I know not of her. Such rumors of me and that distasteful peasant of a woman are vague conversations. They are pure non sense.

BROTHER

A sensitive subject my brother it is to speak of her. My brother, my brother, they nature I admire however, thy curiosity and vanity for such insipid conversation is appalling to me. I beg of thee not to lose thy humor.

ACT II SCENE I

KATHERINA

Have thou noticed what is happening, my lady? **(She asks).**

ELIZABETH

Have I missed something, lady Katherina.

KATHERINA

Look at the helicopter, that's him!

ELIZABETH

Is it the prince of hearts?

KATHERINA

Have thou ever been inside a big boat before, my lady?

ELIZABETH

Only once, I dreamed of many things. But now, I leave it up to the mystery between him and I. Lovely! Isn't it? The boat, I mean. Have thou been inside their large vessel? Lady Katherina.

KATHERINA

Thy excitement for him is lost in thy mind. Dreaming, aren't thou?

ELIZABETH

Tell me about him the prince. Mystical, isn't him?

KATHERINA

Indeed, he is. The rumor today is that his heart belongs to no one. He is into both sexes.

ELIZABETH

Lady Katherina, thou are saying, man and woman? Nay… He is always alone.

KATHERINA

I warn thee he is a ladies' killer.

ELIZABETH

How could it be? I have envisioned him as an angel, not a womanizer. There were times, I saw him sitting in front of me with an expression of authority, settle, gentle, and caring. I could never imagine such unpleasant nature in him.

KATHERINA

Was it a dream, or a meditation? Has thy happiness disappeared with thy love for him?

ELIZABETH

No, it was on a meditation. I closed my eyes and there he was as vivid as life itself. He came into my dream. It was him, I know.

KATHERINA

Thy bare hands actually touch him?

ELIZABETH

Nay, I felt his presence touching my body. It was like a quantum reality in an unexpected moment. I felt his love and presence before me, as, if I had touched him with my mind. I can feel his body and soul. Then, just like that, he became invisible before my eyes. "The invisible Prince of heart".

KATHERINA

Is that how thee see him? Thy expression of love and emotions resembles that of a tantric lover.

ELIZABETH

A tantric Lover! I know not of such terms. Embarrass as I am. A woman of my age, I have no familiarity

with those terms of love. Enlighten me my dear lady
Katherina, enlighten me.

KATHERINA

O dear, how do I put it, in India, in the history of
Goddesses, they were known to be temptress of love.
They are goddesses who used their bodies to dance
and be provocative for man and kings. They were
temptress of love. Lovers of the night!

ELIZABETH

Temptress! O my, is that what I am. At my age, who
would have thought? Of course, experience cannot be
improvised. Can it?

KATHERINA

Thy appearance hinders thy age. At least twenty
years.

ELIZABETH

I thank thee for such a compliment. I need such
gallant expressions in my life. Divorced, in love with
a prince, and broken hearted. And now, I am a tantric
goddess. O might, have I rediscover myself?

KATHERINA

Broken hearted? But thy knowledge of the prince is
an invisible reality. I hardly think the eleven years of

marriage had an impact upon thy sensitivity for man if at all!

ELIZABETH

I know of him in my heart. I was unaware of who he was, a prince. I thought for one moment, I was going to have a heart attack. Never had I felt such impulses for a man before. Never! He is like a mad fever inside my head and my heart with an infectious passion which makes love burn inside me.

KATHERINA

O… dear! Thou are my lady bitten by the love bug as they say. I think thou are simply lost between love and an infatuation for a young prince. What a life, what a life.

ELIZABETH

My heart has spoken words of love from the moment I felt his presence before me. I felt him inside my heart. I did. Lady Katherina, I did.

KATHERINA

I conceive such thoughts go be of illusive nature. Thou are really living in a dream. How romantic thy notion of love? However, it is a bit naïve, I will say, my lady.

ELIZABETH

My words are the pure sounds of my heart beat. If love is what they call this, then let it flow with nature. Such feelings have I never express for other lovers.

KATHERINA

Lovers! Doth thou mean there are others besides the prince?

ELIZABETH

Have I ever told thee about my Indian actor; He is the one who stole my heart in India.

KATHERINA

Keeping secrets from me doth no favor to thee, my lady. Who is that other man? I can barely wait to hear about him. Tell me, tell me!

ELIZABETH

He is a very rich and opulent gentleman from Indian, my lady Katherina.

KATHERINA

He is? Is he of the Arab world?

ELIZABETH

Absolutely not!

KATHERINA

Such certainty doth thy words carry. Tell me my dearest, who is he?

ELIZABETH

The truth is my lady; I do not know him. I know that his presence came to me while I visited India. He is an actor.

KATHERINA

Nay… Is this another vision of love at a distance.

ELIZABETH

I call it a spooky reaction at a distance. It is real my lady, it is real. Einstein called this impossible. Thus, today, I have experience the reality of what communication at a distance truly is.

KATHERINA

Such vague ideas about love from a woman of thy age seems completely delusional. I shall find thee a real man.

ELIZABETH

If only thy imagination could understand the truth of what love is. God have sent me here to fill my heart with love from all three men.

ELIZABETH-DAYDREAMING V. O.

Like a tantric queen, I cry myself to sleep with the sound of music in search of his love inside of me. Tears and sadness of love despair my soul in search of answers. I scape deep into my emotions imagining thy presence with my eyes closed. I hear the sun, the moon and the air whisper words of love to me. These words speak to me of love. Who are thou who possess my heart, who are thou? Are thou a ghost, a spirit of the past, or simply God in his mystical world of faith.

ACT II SCENE II

THE PRINCE

Have I not told thee today how much I love thee?
Hum… My little one.

LITTLE COUSIN

Uncle Please, stop! I wish to go and play with my
friends. May I? Please…

NATALIE- THE SERVANT

Good morning gentleman! May I bring thee some tea,
or coffee?

THE PRINCE

Please Ms. Natalie would you bring tea and coffee for
my guest. He pauses. Here comes my brother.

BROTHER

Good morning! Is everyone ready for another
fantastic adventure? To the desert it is today. The heat
is up. Make sure thou bring enough water.

THE PRINCE

See thee downstairs.

FRIEND

I heard he is being following the old woman. He is curious about her.

THE PRINCE

He what! I despise such the idea of inquisition. **Father enters.**

LITTLE COUSIN

Here comes father, says the little one.

FATHER

Good morning to all! How was your night? I have all the vehicles ready for a trip to the desert. I will be in my office, if anyone needs me. Come, little one. "He is holding her by the hand."

ELIZABETH (V. O.)

She is gasping for air, I cannot breathe. I feel as if I am emerging with thee inside the deep blue sea. Thy presence before me is real. I feel nothing, but the waves of the sea touching my body as I softly flow with, the current. In this moment, I have stop breathing in hope that life will end and take me to another place in time. I feel death come upon me. But something as strong as thy soul has awakened me from death. I have ceased to be hoping that my feelings for thee will disappear. I have succeeded not at such an endeavor. Thus, to my life with thee I return again! I bounce my head back and forth with a sense of passion that takes me deep into a spiritual trance I can't explain. Is it thee, I ask? I know thou are here with me. "My invisible prince"! It is thee, my dearest prince.

ENTER THE PRINCE

Katherina darling! I wonder how thy husband got so lucky to find thee. I desire a woman like thee for a thousand years. Thou are of inexplicable beauty, smart, kind and of very calm nature. My brother is a lucky man. It should have been I.

KATHERINA

Indeed, he is my prince. If only thy constant need for pleasure will cease to be for other woman, thy love for me would have been of pure and perfect pleasure. Don't thou agree?

THE PRINCE

May I remind thee that my love bares not distinction. Have no doubt. It is thee I love, lady Katherina. I like to extend my invitation for a helicopter ride on Saturday. This time, I have like both to come with me.

KATHERINA

I thank thee, your majesty. I will let Ralph know.

BACK TO THE DESERT

BROTHER

Fear not my friends. I am an expert in the desert.
Night is about to fall on us. We will be camping the
night over. Get comfortable. Sorry. No showers in the
desert. Mosquito bite, scorpions, and snakes will all
be present with us.

IBRAHIM

Thy sense of humor is grand my dearest cousin.
Thus, in the presence of the lady's, I consider such
comments rather inappropriate.

BROTHER

Fear me not ladies. Let us start the fire and all evil
will be spell at once. Desert creatures do not like the
heat.

DIANNE

Now, I am nervous.

BROTHER

Don't worry about anything. I am here to protect thee.
I am the desert king, a scorpion in the night.

ANN

Worry not about me. I enjoy the outdoors and fear no creatures of the wild. (She smiles, flirting.)

BROTHER

Are thou worried, Dianne?

DIANNE

Nay…

BROTHER

Hey… are thou biting thy nails?

DIANNE

Are we really sleeping out in the open? And no, I am not biting my nails, I am just a bit nervous.

ANN

Dianne, thou can sleep with me and we'll protect each other.

BROTHER

The two little babies can sleep together. That is, if thou desire. The rest of us will just chat all night long. Go on, go to sleep, my sleeping beauties.

DIANNE

Obvious as it may seem; thou are starting a fight.

BROTHER

Me, start a fight? No madam.

DIANNE

The prince, doth he quarrels with thee some times?

BROTHER

Quarrel? No... We are brothers. We just argued about nonsense. We compete with cars, women, and horses. Here comes one of my best kinsmen.

IBRAHIM

Sir, are the ladies comfortable? Is dinner about to be serve in the desert?

BROTHER

I am just waiting my dearest man.

IBRAHIM

Turn up the gas tank. Let's start the party. Do I see a scorpion? I am joking with thee. I like to get thy attention, beautiful ladies.

ANN

Thy enthusiasm is contagious Ibrahim. Thou just got here and the party has lightened up.

IBRAHIM

Ladies just sit and enjoy the weather. The moon will start to shine right about six o'clock. Then the night will turn into a breathtaking beauty.

DIANNE

Ibrahim, thy nature is kind and caring. If I may I ask, are thou single? Doth a man of such character most have all the ladies following after thee.

IBRAHIM

Nay, to the contrary. My brother here is the gentleman killer. His cars are like magnet to women all over the Middle East.

BROTHER

Thou mean, not my body. I thought it was my body they like. (He says with a very masculine demeanor.)

IBRAHIM

Thou are very well aware of their liking for thee.

BROTHER

Brother, brother, what are thou up to? These ladies will get a wrong impression of me.

FACEBOOK- THE PRINCE

O, the arrogance of that woman. How could she go to Facebook and actually befriend me. I want to know at once who is using my name to follow through. Who?

ELIZABETH -FACEBOOK

In a moment of solitude, I disappear only to find thee. I am thy lover, thy mistress, thy servant and thy mother all in one. And thou are my master. I find my strength as I lose my power and become weak in thee.

THE PRINCE

Mohammed, send someone to know all about this woman. I want to know why she is getting into my private life. How is she bypassing the security?

MOHAMMED

Sir, thou will not believe who is doing this.

THE PRINCE

Who, who?

MOHAMMED

Sir, it was lady Katherina, thy brother's wife.

THE PRINCE

Bloody hell! What is going on? Katherina! Thou are referring to Lady Katherina, our lady Katherina? Tell me that I hear not of such rumors from her. Tell me more Mohammed.

THE PRINCE-ON PHONE

Katherina my darling, how are thou?

KATHERINA

Hello darling, my Prince. How are thou today? It is nice of thee to have call me.

THE PRINCE

I am doing very well until now. May I ask of thy knowledge of the old woman who is tagging me on social media?

KATHERINA

I vaguely know of her. Why, sir?

THE PRINCE

I understand that she has befriended thee. Is this the reason why she knows of me now?

KATHERINA

I would hardly think so, my dearest prince.

THE PRINCE

Don't hide the truth from me Mrs. Katherina. I will find out. I have my ways. Doubt me not. For I have all the power a man can speared.

KATHERINA

I Know very little of her. Personally, I think she is not very well in her head. Doth thy interest in this lady is the purpose for thy call to me, my prince.

THE PRINCE

I have no interest in her. My purpose is merely to keep my life private from the public. I wish not to speak of her. My security is my interest at hand. Speak thee not of me to that woman. Is that clear, my princess.

KATHERINA

But thou are the heart breaker. Aren't thou?

THE PRINCE

Have I broken thy heart ever, lady Katherina?

KATHERINA

Not mine. Mine is taken. I know of many, including the old lady.

THE PRINCE

I detest such words Lady Katherina. I just don't know of her. My life is private. She seems to have a way about her to break all the rules. **He pauses,** then, continues. Are we on for the helicopter right Saturday?

KATHERINA

Indeed, we are my Prince. Thou are most kind, my prince. See thee Saturday.

THE PRINCE

My curtesy I extend to thee as a family member. O, Mrs. Katherina, I understand the old lady is going on a trip to Nepal. Would thee please find out all thou are capable of knowing about her?

KATHERINA

News travels fast my dearest prince.

THE PRINCE

I know more than thou can possibly imagine, my lady. Thy husband told me. Good bye!

STUDIO AT THE PALACE

THE PRINCE

Leave the room and close the door. He says to Natalie, the servant.

STUDIO-LIBRARY

ELIZABETH- ON FACEBOOK

Take me into thy mystical world, my prince. Possess me with all thy mighty power and with all thy heart. Love me, for I have discovered love in thee. I want to lose my senses and become weak in thee. Release me from the shackles of my slave love where I am entangled into a web of passion I can only feel in my dreams. Release me, my prince. Set me free.

BROTHER

Brother, is that thou? What has become of thee? It is late night. Prayer time is coming soon. Thou are up all night? My beloved, what is keeping thee up all night? Social Media, this is so unlike thee.

THE PRINCE

Nothing, I am just reading.

BROTHER

Tell me that is not Katherina. I heard thou are disappointed with her.

THE PRINCE

Now, how in the bloody hell doth thou hear anything about me. How? Is my life no longer private to me?

BROTHER

There are no secrets in our family. Cousin Ibrahim told me about it.

THE PRINCE

Good night my brother. I shall go rest in a moment. Farewell my brother.

BROTHER

Aren't thou the least concern about choosing a bride? Are thou aware of the rumor of thee being gay?

THE PRINCE

I have had enough of innuendoes and rumors. This secret society with norms up their... disgust me! I have had it! It is time for me to go away. I am going to Africa. I need time to breathe. The status of a prince is a demand for rumors and doubts. This has come about because I have chosen a bride. Now, I am a man of worldly nature. It sickens me to have others judge me. I have suffered for love. I have suffered endlessly.

BROTHER

Don't take it to heart. They are just rumors, just rumors. I understand thy suffering for the love of Cousin, Fatima. But father approved not of her. I am sorry, my beloved brother. I am sorry. Love will find thee one day. It is out there looking for thee as well.

ELIZABETH-FACEBOOK

ELIZABETH

"Love is in the air". Tame me like a trainer will tame a lioness. My passion runs high through my veins, and my patience is short. I am the passionate beast thou are looking for. Hold me in thy arms forever. I long for thy love, my Prince of hearts. Thou are my Arab prince of hearts, a fearless being, a chosen man of God, Allah. Sami Allahu le man ha me dah. Allah listens to the one who praise him.

ACT 11 SCENE III

EARLY MORNING

DRIVER

Sir, your majesty, the load is ready. We can go anytime.

THE PRINCE

Let's go! We have a long way to drive. Have all the food and drinks loaded?

DRIVER

Yes, Your majesty, all in. The sun starts to shine early in the Kalahari Desert. We are about six hours away, is the camera ready sir?

THE PRINCE

Set to go. We have a week of fun. Just thee and I. Love the desert, the quiet and wild life. Let's go hunting.

ACT III-SCENE 1

COFFEE-SHOP-OUTDOORS

ELIZABETH

Lady Katherina, I just saw him sitting before me at the coffee shop. There he was. The slender figure I know. He hides his face beneath a baseball cap. But my heart, my heart jumps the minute he walked in. I know it was him. O Katherina. I love him so. How could this be I, a hopeless romantic in love with a prince, and he could be my child. I am twice his age. I should be ashamed!

KATHERINA

Are thou sure it was him? It could of being anyone.

ELIZABETH

My heart never lies. I feel his presence. He touches me with his heart. I feel his energy next to mine. What is it about him Katherina? Tell me. Please, I want to know more about him, my prince.

KATHERINA

Why don't we meet for lunch? I will see thee tomorrow at eleven in the morning. I will tell thee all about him. Sleep well my lady. Sleep well.

ELIZABETH

The curiosity is killing me. I will not sleep. I will wait all night until I know of him.

KATHERINA

Hang in there, darling. It will soon be over.

ELIZABETH

Over! Thou mean I have a chance? Or a dead dream? Which one?

KATHERINA

I will see thee tomorrow. Sleep well, my tantric queen.

ELIZABETH- V.O.

I vaguely consider myself a tantric temptress. Tantric lover me, a temptress, is that what I did dancing for the Guru? Was I being a temptress? She covers her mouth with her hands, and laughs with a giggle.

KATHERINA

Ralph my darling; have thou heard the news about the tantric lover who is after the prince? The word is that she is a spirit from the past chasing him. I have met her. Her story of love for the prince tells me that she is a tantric lover. Rumors are that she dances for her

Guru in India, and he say she is not of this time. She is a spirit of the past.

RALPH

She sounds interesting. I want to meet this lady.

KATHERINA

Have I awakened thy temptation for a temptress, my love?

RALPH

I know the story of temptress in the Indian mythology, but I have never met one. The idea intrigues me. That is all.

KATHERINA

Fear not my love. My heart is open to share thy love if, that tis what thy heart desires.

RALPH

The idea is appetizing. Doth my darling wishes to share as well?

KATHERINA

I believe that freedom is a way of expressing our love. No one is caged to be in love with one. Sharing is freedom and trust.

RALPH

I knew I have chosen the perfect one for me.
Thy understanding of man and their freedom is
provocative and pleasing to me, my darling Katherina,
I love thee forever. I mean forever.

THE FOLLOWING WEEK

BROTHER

Brother, where are thou? Mom is worry about thee.
I have to leave for London. We need thy presence at
home by next week.

THE PRINCE

My journey will end in a day. I will soon be home. I
send kisses to all. I love thee, my brother.

BROTHER

Love thou as well, my brother. Don't kill too many
wild beasts. Bring some lovely photos back.

ELIZABETH

Katherina, tell me what of him? My crazy mind never
stops thinking of him. Is he sexy, caring, loving. Tell
me about him.

KATHERINA

Why so much love for a man of different status than
thou are, why? He is never pleased with one, my
lady. He is a man of many tastes. Thy kinder love
cannot understand his nature. (**Ignorant woman, she
whispers).**

ELIZABETH

I scape from reality to go in places far away to forget
about this madness of love, yet, his thoughts and his
spirit follow me around. I see his face everywhere and
in every man I see on the streets. I don't know what to
do, lady Katherina. Help me forget him. Help me!

KATHERINA

Perhaps thou are suffering from delusion or a sycosis
of the mind or lack of sex thereof.

ELIZABETH

I believe not. One cannot possibly have emotions
for something that isn't real. I never noticed him
before. Everyone has an opinion of what they don't
understand. Besides, lady Katherina, he is not even
my type. I prefer a handsome and intelligent white
man. I find him timid, insecure and too young to
know about a real woman like I. I think I despise him.
I have not chosen this. I think God did.

KATHERINA

O… dear, is it love and hate at the same time. Or are we talking past karma. I really wish I could arrange a meeting with thee and him. Maybe one day. One day Ms. Tantric lady, thou will meet him.

ELIZABETH

Mrs. Katherina, please bring not my hopes up high. For I know that he prefers a younger breed and beautiful models. Those are the rumors. Perhaps he prefers a Muslim woman, one of his own cover from head to toes.

KATHERINA

Thy sense of humor tickles me to death. I think thou are in need of some good squeezing or some good loving. **(She says smiling).**

SATURDAY MORNING-SKY DIVING SCENE-DUBAI

THE PRINCE

Brother, as always, it is a pleasure to set a match with thee here.

BROTHER

The pleasure is mine, brother, after all the
entertaining and putting up a face for the audience all
week long. I will go crazy not to have some fun.

THE PRINCE

I heard the party last night was wild with my cousin,
lady Katherina and the soccer players. Much liquor I
understand.

BROTHER

All the rules of sacrilegious nature were broken last
night. I admit that my guilty pleasure sickens me. I
hope my wife hears not of my immoral acts.

THE PRINCE

It isn't thy bride I fear, but father. He will be disgusted
at knowing thy actions. Not worries, my brother, I can
keep a secret.

ACT IV-SCENE I

GUESTS

Toast to the Prince.

A toast! Hip, hip parade…

DRIVER

Sir, lady Katherina awaits thee in the library.

THE PRINCE

Thank to thee, thou are of most kind nature. Might,
I nearly miss the parachute as I was falling down.
Thanks to Allah for a backup. Alhamdulillah's!

CELEBRATION IN PROGRESS-
ENTERS KATHERINA

Lady Katherina, what a pleasure it is to see thee.
What brings thy presence to my palace?

KATHERINA

Speak thee not as a stranger to me. Thou are very
aware of my presence. Thy eyes do not deceive thee,
my prince. I have seeing the way thy anxious heart
desires me.

THE PRINCE

But lady Katherina, thou are like family to me. I
think not of such immortal actions against my brother
anymore.

KATHERINA

Worry not my dear. Ralph and I, we hold not secrets
to each other. I am a free spirit and so is he.

THE PRINCE

Make me sin not woman of beauty and pleasure. For I
have desire thee since the first day I lay eyes on thee.
I embrace thy presence when thou are near me. This
is not the safest place in the palace. Follow me, lady
Katherina. Follow me to my private hiding place.
Come!

KATHERINA

I can't Harley restrain myself from touching thee,
your majesty. I have dreamed of this moment for
a very long time. Kiss me with thy lips of warm
September air in a hot summer desert night. Kiss me!

THE PRINCE

Thy beauty, lady Katherina is irresistible. Is this what
love feels like? For I have never ever loved a woman
before. Teach me how to love, lady Katherina. Teach
me.

KATHERINA

Thou are the prince of the Arab world, and many come to thy feet for love and pleasure. How is it that thy heart hath never felt love? Thou are not a virgin prince, are thou! Are thou a ghost, a spirit or the missing part of me? She says laughing.

THE PRINCE

Thou are the copulate of love, pleasure and sin all together in one. Thy presence evokes a sexual appetite that even a man of faithful nature cannot resist. Why are thou so sensual, Katherina? Why? And no, I am not a virgin. My share of ladies I have had. In love with another I am not.

KATHERINA

O... I see. Thou are a shy prince. Innocence is beauty. Taketh me in thy arms and hold me tight. I will show thee what is like to love. Hold me tight, closer my prince, closer.

THE PRINCE

I have had my count of ladies, but none, none are like thee, my lady Katherina. I feel the passion from thy beauty cometh to me from every angle of thy body. The old lady hath not beauty to compare to thee. Thou are a tantric queen, a goddess of love thou are. Let me make love to thee like no one has ever loved thee before. Let me be the one to love thee eternally. O lady Katherina. He whispers in her ears.

KATHERINA

Bring no thy thoughts of this woman into our moments of passion. This is our moment, my prince, lie on the bed, and let me rest my head upon thy shoulders for a moment. Let me love thee once again with all the passion left in me for tonight.

THE PRINCE

Worry not my lady Katherina, for I have left the party on the false pretenses of an emergency. To thee I belong all night. Tempt me once again with thy sensual body touch me with thy hands of love. Touch me. Yes, lady Katherina, love me like no one has ever done before. Thy magic I feel in my heart, my soul and all my senses. Yes, my darling, thou are the temptation I have been seeking for. If evil exist in me. Tonight, it has visited the doors of my heart. Love me forever my beautiful temptress. Love me.

KATHERINA

Not so quick my lady lover. She removes his hands from her private. I know thou are full of energy and passion. I to have a man of my own and nothing last forever. This moment we shall treasure. Tomorrow have yet to come.

THE PRINCE

Show me not a side of thy cold nature, lady Katherina. I want to see and experience all of thee. Removed all your clothing at once, I cannot wait to see thy naked beauty. Come let me touch thy body with passion and tenderness. My passion is growing stronger. Thy facial expression suffices my excitement for thee. Come to me my beautiful temptress. Come!

ACT IV SCENCE II

PAKINSTAN-EARLY MORNING

KHAN

All preparations are ready. We will cross the border between Pakistan and India before noon time. I have arranged extra security for thy protection my beloved brother. Malika, our lawyer will be waiting for us at the border. Any question or concerns, my prince?

THE PRINCE

My only concern is the war with India. Today, the newspapers announced the killing of a general from Pakistan in India. If we use a vehicle with a tag from India, it will help us infiltrate without been noticed. I want to leave no chance for mistakes. My people count on me.

KHAN

Fear not my prince. I have always taken care of thy safety and will always put security before all. Fear not, my brother.

THE PRINCE

What was that? Allah!!!! A blast of this magnitude must have taken an entire village out.

KHAN

Here, let's go into this small village until Malika arrives. Come, this way, my prince, this way.

THE PRINCE

Who are these people?

KHAN

They are my people. Our safety is in good hands, my prince. Fallow me to the tunnel. We will stay here for the moment. I am afraid the fight is not over. The boarder hasn't clear yet. We must wait.

THE PRINCE

May I ask what the matter is?

KHAN

Retaliation is common whenever there's an attack between India and Pakistan.

THE PRINCE

My concerns are to be on time for me to meet with the general. If I shall face any inconveniences with time, please alert him of my absence. I will not put my life in danger to mitigate a negotiation. Here, Malika is calling. Please ask what is new out there?

KHAN

Everything is in order my prince. Thou are in Malika's hands. Go on, right alone. The road is secure. Go in peace, my prince, Go in peace.

MALIKA

We will spend the night at the village. I have arranged a massage for tonight. Will my prince need any extra comfort?

THE PRINCE

No, my dear lady. Just the presence of thy beauty will suffice me for the night. Is all I need to calm my nerves tonight.

MALIKA

Is that so my prince, is that so. I heard the news about Laurent. Is it true? Has thy heart finally been taken a lover of thy chosen? I will not say she is a fortunate one. For I have no deed or obligations to thee. I enjoy thy pleasures immensely my prince.

THE PRINCE

Fear not my darling. The eyes of the beholder cannot see reality. My heart is not with her, but another. My sadness I cannot hide from my eyes. Perhaps thou can help me forget the deep sorrow in my soul. Promised me Malika that I can have thy friendship forever? I suspect thou are spying on me. Not one in my family knows of her. No one except, my father.

MALIKA

We are more than friends my prince. We are lost and found lovers. Thy presence penetrated my soul and it has never, ever left me. Quickly! Remove the head scarf. Remove it now, my prince. We are approaching the border. It will give them a reason to search the vehicle. Remove it at once. Please! I beg of thee.

THE PRINCE

I will not betray our beloved Allah. I cannot do such a demand.

MALIKA

There is only one choice, the scarf or thy live? Choose for me, my prince. Choose quickly. An Arab is not a problem but being a Pakistani in Indian is a death sentence.

THE PRINCE

I will never forgive myself for such act against my God. Allah!!!! I have rather die. "Rab 'bigh firlee", Allah forgive me. He remove his scarf angrily.

MALIKA

We made it! We got in. Thanks god. Go in peace. Thy family will rejoice.

JBR-The Beach Jumeirah-

The Sound of the Engines is loud. The Younger Brother is the Handsome Fast and Furious. Black Car Crashes Against a light Pole.

THE PRINCE

How are thou my brother? We are sick worry about thee? Had thou lost control of the car, or was there another reason.

YOUNGER BROTHER

My inquiries of thee have been for days on. Brother, have thou being hiding from us. No one knows of thy secret getaway or hideaway. I miss thee.

THE PRINCE

Rest well my brother. Father will be here soon. I shall look after thy children and bride. Rest well, my beloved brother.

LITTLE COUSIN

Uncle, uncle, thou have been lost from our presence. I have missed thee for a long time. Mother asks of thee all day and all night. Grandfather will be here soon. Come uncle, let's wait here. "**(The prince nerve's and anxiety begins shows in his demeanor).**"

THE PRINCE

Darling grandpapa is coming. I have to take care of business, the army and all the office necessities. I most go now. Give my love to father.

LITTLE COUSIN

Please don't leave uncle, please stay with me. Please!

THE PRINCE

Darling as much as I would love to stay, I can't. I have to obey the duties of my father. I have to go. Love thee forever. Um! Kisses.

ACT IV- SCENE III

KATHERINA

Have I news to tell thee my lady. We party until the late night. Drunken fool like mad we were.

ELIZABETH

O how lovely lady Katherina. No invitations for me. How I wish I could have seeing his face. Would I ever meet him? Why have thou exempt me from his presence, Why, Lady Katherina?

KATHERINA

Perhaps, next time. This was only family gathering and a last minute invitation. O, did I say we went for a helicopter ride. Yes, it was marvelous, just marvelous.

ELIZABETH

How enchanting it all sounds. I hope one day I can see him up close, in person, just once. Tell me lady Katherina, why doth thy hide me from thy friends? Am I not worthy of thy friends?

KATHERINA V. O.

Old hag, what make thee think thou belong with us? Thou are unlike us, Russians. We do know how to drink.

ELIZABETH

Lady Katherina, until we meet again. I most leave.
My house duties await me. The maid is coming soon.
Good Bye, darling!

KATHERINA

Good Bye!

(V. O.)

If thou only knew that I had him all to myself last
night. Stupid old bag. And there is no reason for the
lack of invitation, just not for thee.

**Saturday Night-Ocean Front- Moon Shining over
the Arabian Sea**

OLDER BROTHER

There! There she is. That's her. O might… she is
beautiful. Car Speed up fast. That is her. Brother, I
cannot believe it. How old?

THE PRINCE

I have no idea. But she looks better than Lady
Katherina. Beauty and grace, and sex-appeal… No
wonder why she hates her. A woman's quarrel is never
about friendship, but competition for a lover, a man.

OLDER BROTHER

What makes thee think she does?

THE PRINCE

Women only argued for one reason. Man, competition, jealousy, nothing else.

OLDER BROTHER

Thou are so lucky to have them fight for thee. I know not of what is like to be wanted by so... many beautiful women, yet thou are not in love. What now my brother. Does thy curiosity bring any interest in her?

THE PRINCE

Speak thee nonsense. I shall have me a virgin to please my father. All else is but play. Toys and dolls, that's what they are.

OLDER BROTHER

May I express my thoughts to thee my brother? I will say that thy bride will not be chosen by love but by merits of the royals. Sad, I feel for thy heart. I know thy heart is not with a beauty of Arabian brides or Lauren. I know.

THE PRINCE

Nonsense! It is father, he objects to my choices.

OLDER BROTHER

Thy choice my brother, are forbidden. One cannot marry thy own blood. Regrets will come in the handicap of a child. I know of thy desire for lady Katherina. Thy need for family closeness keeps thee in proximity with unforbidden love. Thanks to Allah, our brother is of flexible demeanor. A loving king he is.

THE PRINCE

It is my insatiable appetite for their beauty keeps me a prisoner for their desire. My beloved brother, she does have a way with words. Her words bewilder my masculine strength. I feel needed, wanted and appreciate by her.

OLDER BROTHER

I know the truth will come out one day. Thou are a bit attracted to her. Aren't thou?

THE PRINCE

Words are all I admire of her. Her beauty is acceptable, but not my type.

OLDER BROTHER

Brother… brother, lie not to me. For I have known
for a long time how much thy taste for older women
doth thee desire. Regardless of the beauty, thy comfort
in love belongs with an older woman. For what is a
virgin to a worldly man? They all cry for thee and
love thee. How fortunate thou are my prince of hearts.
Go for love and not beauty. For their beauty will fade,
but love will remain forever!

THE PRINCE

Thy words of comfort I taketh to my heart. Except
that now, I have no one to love but my forbidden love.

READING ROOM- I-PHONE.

Status doth not recognize the heart or emotions of a
stranger who is weak before thy presence. Thy image
I see my prince in everything that breathe around me.
For I bleed like thee, I feel like thee and I too have
a heart feel with love. Why can thy eyes notice my
presence? Is it I, the woman doth thy fear. For I know
with certainty that thou are a man of many pleasures.
Yet, love thy heart knows not of. Could love abide in
thee my prince? Ever! For I see what no one else can
see in thee. I know thy heart can love. I know.

OLDER BROTHER

Thou are lucky, my brother, I am the handsome one.
How thy nature doth attracts so many beauties near?
Take advantage, for this too shall pass.

THE PRINCE

No bride of mine will change who I am. The chosen
one will have to accept me as I am. I shall remain a
free man.

OLDER BROTHER

How little doth thee know of marriage and family
commitment. I too once thought I will be free, Then,
the little ones. They changed my life forever. And
here I am a married man, children and all. One day,
my brother, one day.

THE PRINCE

O, how noble thou are my brother. Unlike thee, I am
a brave soldier. One who lives with desires and will
fight for his family honor until death. Life endeavors
more than we can bear to understand.

ACT V- SCENE I

INDIAN ACTOR

Prince, your majesty! I have noticed the images of the older woman, how now?

THE PRINCE

O… nonsense, they all seek monetary redemption from me. But none have succeeded.

INDIAN ACTOR

Thy heart has yet to be touched by the scent of a real woman. I too profess her and make love to her with my mind. It is I who's driving her crazy. Doth she knows vaguely of me.

THE PRINCE

I find thy suggestions preposterous.

INDIAN ACTOR

Her words bring joy and pleasure to my heart. Images of her jump across the screen like an exchange of passionate intentions between her and I.

THE PRINCE

Have thou lost thy mind?

INDIAN ACTOR

Look at her my majesty, look at her! Tell it to my face that thou are not the list interested in her. Tell me! (He whispered in his ears).

THE PRINCE

Please discard such images from my presence, at once.

INDIAN ACTOR

I love all about her. She is sexy, seductive and provocative. To love the unknown is like loving God. Have thy heart ever love at all?

THE PRINCE

Why are thou concern with my life, my privacy? Why? I have lived in this palace for thirty years with many beauties by my side until now. Today all hell is braking lose with one old ugly woman. Thou may have the pleasure to have the old rag to thyself. To thee, I give all of her. Pleasure her with thy mind, my beloved.

INDIAN ACTOR

Nay, nay, my eyes have never seeing such an expression in thy face, your majesty. What troubles thee, my prince?

THE PRINCE

I shall return to my duties for now. Good day, my friend. As usual, it is always a pleasure to have thy presence in our palace. Enjoy thy stay. (He walks away.)

ENTER ELIZABETH

Elizabeth desire for her lover grows stronger and the anxiety brings her to a nervous breakdown. Death falls upon her from lack of connection to her lovers. Her beloved prince begins to crave for her attention, her words, and her photos on social media have suddenly disappeared. Weeks later, she bounces back and forward with words of love to her second beloved, the man of her heart," The Indian Actor". She steals love from both with her charms as they both fall madly in love with her. She teases them like a Goddess of tantric love. She suffers at the thought of meeting her lovers. Her passion and desperation compels her to travel in hope that they will follow her, and they do. They both attempt to reach out, but she misses them every time by minutes. In her despair, she nearly loses her mind.

ENTER THE PRINCE

The prince feelings for lady Katherina are dying, and a new desire is born for the older woman with her gallant expressions to him. The prince has fallen for a woman who swears she will die for him. Now, for the first time, the prince understands what is like to love a woman he never met before. He has fallen in love with this woman like a spooky reaction at a distance. And she is being coerced by lady Katherina and the young fiancé. He now follows her wherever she travels on hope to meet once. The older woman is tormented and torn between the Indian Actor love and her prince of hearts. They are rivals for her love. Her love and expressions gives them power as they feel wanted, loved and admire by her. A new lover has entered into her life. She is now in love with a third man. Confuse by the love of her prince and her indian actor, she begins to seek for spirituality.

ACT V -SCENE II

ELIZABETH

Thy heart has finally recognized thy love for me, my prince. Now, I see in thee the lovely winds of fall. The impetuous heat of the summer and the blissful cold of the winter caress thy face as I breathe my last breath of life here alone. For death hath cometh to proclaim my soul. Now that I breathe in thee and thee in me; my eternal love cannot be denied. Show me the light, my prince. Show me the light into my final destiny in the heavens of thy arms. I want to feel my last breath upon thy masculine bosom. Show me the light. My prince of hearts, show me the light!

THE PRINCE

Thy power has magic to conflict my soul whose light is given me with magnificent gifts of life. Die not my lady, die not. For I too need thy words of hope. I feel emptiness without thy presence. Die not my dearest lady. For I too love thee. Die not in my arms, my beloved. (His words surprises him for a moment. He realizes his hidden feelings for her have finally blossomed into an expression of love).

ELIZABETH

Regret not what thou have taken from me, but that which thou are not within power to face in me, my love for thee. My light, my soul, my power weakens now. Where hath thy beauty of such gallants' statute hidden from my vision? For I, I neither seeing, nor known of thy presence ever, my beloved prince. In a moment of careless whisper, my eyes and heart cut on to thee. Such impression doth thy heart hath upon mine. Who but thee possess such everlasting love poison? Thus, tonight, my beloved, it all comes to end. Fear not my beloved, for I am immortal. I will never die. I will always be with thee.

THE PRINCE

Death shall not taketh thy love from me. Not if I have the power to heal thy soul and broken heart. Breathe life into this world of ours and let me set thee free. Let not thy soul fade away, for I too, feel thy love in me. Return to me my beloved lady. Return to me. He disappears.

ELIZABETH

Lady Katherina, I wasn't expecting thee in this moment. To what do I owe this surprise?

KATHERINA

Words travel fast. It is all in the family. What prompt thy illness my lady. Was it love?

ELIZABETH

Hardly my lady Katherina, I think I lost control of my mind. I had a nervous breakdown. Stress from desperation. I felt death near.

KATHERINA

Sorry to know of thy despair. O, haven't thou heard the news? The prince is in love with a young lad. Finally, he has chosen one, finally!

ELIZABETH

I know not of his personal matter. All I see is images of him on Facebook. I am in love with a ghost, a spirit or a power unlike no other. Perhaps, it is God's love expressing itself to me. Indeed.

KATHERINA

I agree, his presence seems like a magnetic light that attracts all women to him. What kind of man possesses such powerful influences to all female species? I understand that he is very well in doubt like his father. This is the reason why all the ladies pursue him.

ELIZABETH

Lady Katherina, how doth thy knowledge of such a personal matter become known to thee?

LADY KATHERINA

This is no old news. It is well known amongst the Arab ladies. He prefers the young lad. They are more capable of taking him without complain.

ELIZABETH

Thy knowledge of his private life is quite ample, Lady Katherina. I knew not of his well develop nature. Although I have to say…sometimes, his male membrane is visible through his attire. Lady Katherina, be well. (Smiling at her she says).

PALACE ELABORATE LIBRARY- ENTERS THE FATHER

THE PRINCE FATHER

Son, today thou are thirty years old. May I remind thee, that it is time to choose a bride? The behavior will influence many who follow thy passion and character as a prince of the Arab world.

THE PRINCE

Father, please, there is no need to remind me. I know my duty and responsibilities to the people of my region. Worry not, I will never forsake thee, father.

YOUNGER BROTHER

Father, father, thy presence is needed. The Queen of England is here to see thee.

FATHER

I have made myself clear to have free time with the family. This is but an abrupt disruption from my time. I will see her at once. Please advise my secretary this is the last time I will accept any visitors without previous announcement.

YOUNGER BROTHER

I see she is expressing love for another man. Could it be she knows of thy new chosen bride? Come on brother. Thou can do it. Come on! Racing is thy passion.

BROTHER-SAEED

Thou have won my brother, thou are the winner. Thou have done us proud. Congratulations, congratulations, Mumtaz! Mabrouk! Another great polo match for the Arab Prince.

THE PRINCE

Look at my Facebook page. One photo of the Polo trophy and all the ladies are going crazy. I love it! Can you see, it is magic, magic is what I create, isn't it? I tease them with images and they all fall for it. Let's celebrate.

DRIVER

My prince, thy presence is demanded at the library of thy father.

A DAY LATER- MAIN LIVING ROOM

THE PRINCE

To what do I owe the pleasure? Father.

FATHER

My concerns are simply about the use of liquor. May I have the driver available? I want not public scenes of misbehavior. I understand thy need for celebrating, thus, thou are responsible for all actions. Please be delinquent.

THE PRINCE

Father, please, may I remind thee that I am a mature man. A man at my age desires not to hear such words of repressions. I thank thee for thy concern, my beloved. Good bye, father.

ELIZABETH POETIC THOUGHTS

I feel a sense of despair for her careless talk over me, my thought do not deceive me. I think she is in love with him. My intuitions do not lie to me. At a glance, we can see Elizabeth dance to the sound of Arab music on the radio. Tears fall to her cheeks. Sadness she expresses into a melancholic feeling about her beloved prince. She dances her anguish away to the point of exhaustion, then falls to sleep.

ENTERS THE PRINCE
FATHER LATE NIGHT

FATHER

I warned thee of thy actions in public. Thy actions have caused the royals much grievance of reputation. I am unable to put into words what my heart feels for the family of this child in the hospital. He is now in a coma. Consumption of alcohol is forbidden in our religion. How will I explain this, how? Allah! Forgive thee. Rab" bigh firlee!

BROTHER

Father, the reporters are here. They are demanding an explanation to what has happen? Should I send them away?

FATHER

I will take care of it. I have to face it or else, innuendos will arise from all false sources of media and their lies. I will protect my family at all cost. Now, son, please leave the house or leave the country temporarily.

REPORTER

May we know what happened?, your highness? How is the child, is he dead or alive?

FATHER

We are taking care of the situation and the family one hundred percent. It was an accident. Nothing else, he didn't see the child. May I be excuse now?

REPORTER

Sir! Sir! Is the baby going to live? He is in a coma as we speak. Will he live?

FATHER

No one knows the outcome, only Allah knows the answer. Good day to all!

SECURITY AT THE DOOR No more questions. We are done! Leave please! Leave!

ACT V-SCENE III

We will stop in Thailand. I have to meet a friend.

PILOT

Your majesty, are we meeting Tania, your friend, the lawyer?

THE PRINCE

Indeed, my friend, indeed.

Where shall we dine my lady?

TANIA

Your majesty, thy heart shows not peril for the harm caused to the child.

THE PRINCE

News spreads fast, doesn't it, Miss Tania. I vaguely record the accident. Shall we eat now, Tania? I have a few hours to speared, then, I must leave.

TANIA

Try this, it is delicious. Agreed?

THE PRINCE

Indeed it is. What is it?

TANIA

Is a love poison, for lovers only?

THE PRINCE

Is that an invitation Tania?

TANIA

Thou be the judge. A few hours is all we have.

THE PRINCE

It's such a pleasure to see thee Tania, always.

TANIA

Tell me my prince of hearts, who doth thy love?

THE PRINCE

If I shall tell thee the truth with certainty and confidence, can I trust thy intentions? My heart has not been romance by cupid. For love simply is misinterpreted with insatiable words in need to love one, but not thyself.

TANIA

Is it a Muslim woman, the young lad?

THE PRINCE

Don't be foolish, my views of this world are not of the old. I am a modern man. I will choose as I please. She is a French beauty.

TANIA

Who is she? Tell me my dear prince.

THE PRINCE

No one has captured my heart. Not even thou has ever! Thy love I will cherish until the day I die. No one is capable of understanding me or accepting my ways. Our relationship is pure passion.

TANIA

Your highness, such words of ingratitude thou express about love. Is thy honesty as visible as thy soul? I could hardly imagine thee exposing thy soul to anyone.

THE PRINCE

In matters of the heart, one plus one not always equals two. At times it equals three. Women, they are always trying to figure things out. Aren't thou?

TANIA

Such vague ideas of reality doeth thou have.

THE PRINCE

I have no time to be in love but to be loved. Yet only one has captured my attention lately. But she is taken. She is a married woman.

TANIA

But that should not stop who thou are. I know thy needs and wants are always met.

THE PRINCE

I cannot make my brother's wife my mistress.

TANIA

Your brother's wife! Thou are in love with her. Oh… might! How could thy careless heart fall for such forbidden love. How my dearest prince, how?

THE PRINCE

What is love but a thief that taketh and steals blindly in a moment of careless passion? Love is a battle field of the hearts.

TANIA

If thou are not careful, my prince, thy heart could be served in a gold platter.

THE PRINCE

I know, I have betrayed my brother's trust. I have allowed my passion to possess my spirit, thus a forbidden love of my brother's wife, Katherina.

TANIA

I express no remorse for thy actions. My heart is crushed.

THE PRINCE

Why doth thou have high expectations of me. I have never confessed love or made promises to thee I cannot keep. Our relationship is pure act of passion in the moment.

TANIA

I must leave my dear prince. My child awaits me before bedtime. It is always a pleasure to share my emotions with thee. (Her sadness she hides from her face as she turns her back to him). She then walks away slowly with feminine seduction.

THE PRINCE

We shall meet again, my dear Tania. Good bye!

THE PILOT

May I wish thee a pleasant evening, Tania.

THE PRINCE

Tania and I are dear friends. The distance doth not allow us to share more passion. Besides, I belong to no one, no one. (He repeats).

THE PRINCE- V. O.

This old woman is to me pure platonic curiosity. Yet, her presence intrigues me like no other. Why, I ask myself, why a Love triangle? I have taken a liking to this woman. Her age is that of my mother. Yet, to me, it matters not. Here, a new post from Turkey. Change the flight plan, to Turkey I am going.

THE PRINCE-V.O. CONTINUE

Dance lady of seduction, thy sensual expression I desire like a hungry wolf. Thy appeal of sensual moves allures my desire like a hot summer day in the desert, sweating with passions of love. Dance my lady, dance for me. Indeed, a temptress thou are. I will take thee to places unknown to thee. I will shower thee with love and gifts like a princess. Dance my temptress lover. I love thee in silence and secrecy from all. Why the tears, why? Doth thy heart sense my presence before thee, for I can only see thee at a distance? If my invitation thou accept, my heart belongs to thee tonight. Accept my love tonight and I shall possess thy mind, body and soul forever.

ELIZABETH

Thy presence I feel my prince of hearts. Is it thee indeed? I can feel thy heart beating next to mine. My desperation and happiness together brings me to tears as the prayer time calls forth. Is it thee or is God calling me before his command. Please reveal thyself to me. My heart is in pain with a sensation, perhaps mistake by love. Is it the love of God or thou are calling upon me. I want to become one with thee. My heart is on fire and the madness in my mind extends to all the ending nerves of my body. I feel thy touch, yet I see not thy hands. I feel thy kisses yet, I see not thy lips. Thou are the one I love with every fiver of my body, my cells and my heart beat as I live for thee in this magical moment of love.

THE PRINCE

My heart doth thee sense, but my intentions thou are unable to read. Yet, my desires for thy presence doth thy missed. Indeed, thou are claiming to know of me, but understanding lack thee of the truth of who I am.

NEW SCENE -LADY KATHERINA

Oh… dear, not feeling so good.

RALPH

What is wrong my love?

LADY KATHERINA

Have to pay a visit to the doctor. Is it morning sickness, my darling?

RALPH

It has been five years since we have try. Now our efforts are over. Have we finally harvest our fruits, my love?

LADY KATHERINA V. O.

Of course darling, nothing will please me more than to know we have done it. Thou are but a careless fool. Thy soul is blind. This is not the fruit of thy labor. A gift from the prince indeed, it is. How I would like to weep for thee. My joy is greater than my regrets. My love bares the fruit of the one capable whose baron is not.

RALPH

It is such a joy to know my darling, such a joy.

ON PHONE-THE PRINCE

And how are thou today my lady Katherina, My princess.

KATHERINA

Sick in the morning as a wounded lioness. After all, I blame it on the blasphemy, liquor and good times, my prince.

THE PRINCE

Doth any suspicion awaken in my brother?

LADY KATHERINA

Nay, not the least. My prince, thy head he would have without concern. Thy nature he resents very much.

THE PRINCE

How much do I desire thee now? Can we scape for a moment?

KATHERINA

I will visit with my friend, the old lady. I shall see thee in two hours.

THE PRINCE

Anxiously I wait for thee. My beloved.

LADY KATHERINA

All I ask of thee is to truly swear of thy love for me.

THE PRINCE

My beloved lady Katherina, I treasure thee with every
ounce of blood in me. I know, I know, I have sin and
betrayed my brother. How can my love doubt thee, my
lady? "May Allah forgive me for such vain thoughts, I
beg of him.

LADY KATHERINA

He blesses thee for baring fruits for thy brother. He
forgives thee for thy transgression, and loves thee, for
thou are his favor.

THE PRINCE

Thy news is music to my heart. What a pleasure, what
a pleasure! Stay with me longer, my beloved. Stay
with me for the night.

LADY KATHERINA

My complaints of morning sickness cannot delay my
telling of the news. I am having twins. Don't forget,
my beloved, he knows not of us. Hiding it will serve
us better for the disappointment could be greater.
Good bye, my beloved.

YOUNGER BROTHER

Good news Allah blesses thee, my brother Ralph.
True duty as a father awaits thee. Congratulations,
congratulations, my beloved brother. Allahandu Allah!

ACT VI-SCENE I

INVISIBLE PRINCE

The constant mystery of their passages marks their love with constant persistence for tears are many which failures outdo. Their path hath not cometh to term with time, thus, the end never cometh between their hearts. What always prevails is not the constant seeking for love, but the dreaming of it coming to be. And thus in the end, love in their hearts is proclaim forever, eternally.

ELIZABETH A POETRY EXPRESSION

Thy innocence bypasses thy putrefy actions of mischievous nature cleansing it with the pureness of love. Thus, who claims such merits? Thee! I! Have I giveth thee a new hope, a new life, my prince? Have I? Many tears of hope have I cry in desperation of thy presence before me. All I see is thee in the beauty of the sky, the moon, in the brilliance of the sun thou are in life like the blood circulating from my heart to thee.

YOUNGER BROTHER

Thy despicable actions have no merits. Are thou ever exhausted of thy behavior or actions my brother?

THE PRINCE

Brother, have thy ears heard any of my expression of me. Doth love exists anymore? Love hears not, fears not, and judges none.

BROTHER

Arrogance possess thee in abundance my beloved brother. Such is certain of thee.

THE PRINCE

Confidence is not for the weak but the strong. For I have acquired it with certainty by competing with man unlike thee.

BROTHER

Why doth thou excel at portraying the worst thy have to offer. If only thou understood what opinions of thee and lady Katherina rumors the palace.

THE PRICNE

I bare no shame for my actions. Those hypocrites's in the palace speakth of me while; they do as they please, but I hide not the truth.

BROTHER

I must leave now. This dialogue displeases my nature.

THE PRINCE

Fear not. Opinions are but judgements of the self. I satisfy not the hypocritical needs of others.

BROTHER

Thy actions are a mere egocentric nature indeed. Thy opinion of joy with whores, liquor and fast cars are but an abomination to the royals. Is it ever enough, my brother? Is it?

THE PRINCE

Indeed, my brother, life has granted me such pleasures and I intend to embrace them all.

BROTHER

My question remains as to why have thou been chosen over any of our brothers. Why are thou deserving of such merits from the royal?

THE PRINCE

I have been chosen by Allah. Neither man or royals can change my gifted nature.

BROTHER

Now, tell me who the ragged woman is?

THE PRINCE

What have prompted thee to ask? She means nothing to me, more than enough beauty waits for me.

BROTHER

I hear something hiding in thy voice. My heart doth not deceive me. I know thee, my brother, I know thee well.

THE PRINCE

Doth thou see love in my eyes?

BROTHER

Love only giveth merits to that which is. It sees not. Love is a vibration of the heart share between two people.

THE PRINCE

I resent the constant inquisitions about me and my private life. My princess awaits me, goodbye my brother.

THE PRINCE AND LAURENT

My beautiful princess to be, how are thou today. Is the palace a pleasant place for thy comfort? I know things are different in Paris.

LAURENT

Come darling… I have an appointment to the spa.
Forgive me for my tardiness. I shall return soon.

THE PRINCE

Darling before thou depart, may I ask about the use of
my name on Facebook to intimidate this Old Woman.
What prompt thy actions, is it jealousy?

LAURENT

Oh, my prince, how is it that thou are so impregnated
with news of this Old Woman? Intuitive creatures we
are. O dear, expressing our emotions is normal with
us women. We all connect at some level.

THE PRINCE

Thy actions Lady Laurent do no good serving to
my reputation. It is imperative that I maintain an
impeccable image. We shall continue this dialogue,
Miss. Laurent.

FATIMA

Brother, may I bring to thy attention that this woman
is spreading rumors about Lady Katherina and the
tweens. She says in social media they belong to thee.

THE PRINCE

I will take care of it, my sister. No one defames my family. Not a deceitful hag like her. How dare! How dare her make such accusations in the Public media about me. Bloody hell!

FATIMA

Brother, thy actions against this evil woman can complicate things for the family, I understand, she is suicidal.

THE PRINCE

Perhaps her actions are false pretenses like all the others. They all seek for status and monetary recompense from our kingdom. Everyone knows we bathe our beloved with treasures of jewels and liverish houses.

FATIMA

My dear brother, thou must know, unlike the others, she is willing to die for thee. She loves thee, my beloved. She truly doth. Why can man die for us, ladies, why?

THE PRINCE

It has been known to me that she fasted for thirty days during Ramadan. She is trying to connect with us spiritually.

SOCIAL MEDIA-PHOTOS OF THE PRINCE- LAURENT POSTED.

LAURENT

Show me thy bosom; it is me, the prince. See my photos, show me thy bosom. Show me now! It is I, the prince. Trust in me.

ELIZABETH

Please my prince I am not sure who thou are. How can I be certain? Is it thee, my prince of hearts? Naïvely she shows her bosom. Then it is display all over Facebook.

LAURENT ON FACEBOOK

ENTER LAURENT AND THE PRINCE

I love thy poem. Thou my lady, are very inquisitive. This kind of love I have never felt. I love thy poems, thy love, thy nature and all thy words of hope to me.

LAURENT

Come to me my beauty of an angel. Come! To what do I own the pleasure of this beautiful diamond neckless, my Prince?

THE PRINCE

It is customary for the royals to rain their princess with gifts and pleasure.

LAURENT

Proud as I am of the beauty God has granted me, it couldn't have been more precious, my prince. I fear not the older woman of lower status than I. My father taught me well.

THE PRINCE

Do I hear despair in thy voice about her, my princess? Why?

LAURENT

Make love to me my prince of hearts. I want to know that thou are mine and only mine. Love me now.

THE PRINCE

Come to me my little princess. One day, I will take thee to the throne. My father and all the royals will treasure thee like a Queen of the Arab World. Thy beauty and wit will exalt all who meet thee. O God lady, why are thou so hot? Doth thy love yearn for me as much as I do? Come to me my beloved. Come to me.

ENTER FATIMA

Laurent, thy actions are in question to the royal. If I am not mistaken, thy actions are more damaging to the reputation of the Prince than thou can imagine. Why Laurent, Why? Thy future position as a queen is now in question by the royal family.

LAURENT

She praises him with explicit words and poems. She doth not belong. I had to stop her.

FATIMA

Laurent my dear, to have been chosen by the Prince is a privilege. Obviously thou doth not recognized such merits. How lucky thou are. Thousands wish upon such merits by the prince. Yet, thou are the one. Thy actions on Facebook against that woman are unacceptable. My heart hurts for thee. Know that broken pieces cannot be mended back together. The damage is done. We take our religion very serious. May Allah forgive thee Laurent?

THE PRINCE

Fatima, have I not right to privacy. Doth the need to converse now, in this moment become a priority to thee? Have thy manners being forgotten?

FATIMA

My darling brother, I think is of best interest to hear what I have to say. It concerns thee the most. Thy reputation is flying all over the internet. Thy future princess hath managed to put thy integrity to question. Take a look!

ELIZABETH

The intellect of an exoteric mind laced with passion, knowledge and evil is who she is my Prince of Hearts. How can I forget thee, now that thou have chosen thy bride? Her portrayal to deception to me with thy name has gained me my reputation as well. My memories will forever hunt me in the hidden corner of my mind. Thus, today, for once my prince, I have decided to step out of my cocoon, and let go of thee. Thou belong to one who has betrayed thy integrity. I shall find refuge in myself. She has deceived thee and me, both. I beg thee to protect thyself. Goodbye, my prince of hearts.

THE PRINCE ON FACEBBOOK

Thy grief is but an internal expression of anger hidden from the emotional outburst of unsatisfied love. Thus such expression of energy taken to the heart, the mind, and the body is but internal torment in thy soul. Smile my lady. Thy soul can fly into an abundance of happiness.

ELIZABETH

Hath thy heart finally softens to love. O my prince of hearts, tell me that my love hath finally touched thee. The prince who once belong to all like a succulent bird whose sweets nectars he extracts from all the flowers never to be satisfied. Tell me that thou hath cometh to me at last, my prince of hearts.

ACT VII SCENE I

ENTER OLDER BROTHER

Sinners aren't we all. Thy nature is not different than that of an animal. Finish the bottle of vodka. Go ahead and drink thee thy sadness into unconsciousness. For many have suffer in thy name without thy regards for their pain. How long will thy need to please women will last, how long my brother? Doth thy heart speak to thee of thy true love? Tell me thy honest secret, my brother. Tell me.

THE PRINCE

Leave me alone brother. This journey of marriage is not an easy choice. I will take Laurent by the hand to please my father's desires, but my heart belongs to the unknown. She is the one who has changed my heart. I owed her my new life. She hath taught me how to love. Thus, I confess, I love her. I will marry another. Happiness abides not in me now. For today, I wish death upon me than to make the decision I have to make. I have suffered much in silence. My story of love differs not from hers. For I have loved two women. Neither of which I can have.

OLDER BROTHER

But why not my brother, why can thou have them? Take thy love not in vain. This will hunt thee until the end of day.

THE PRINCE

Thy ears have not heard a word I said. Royalty and love do not go hand in hand. One must choose for the sake of royal status, not love. I wish I had not been chosen to be a prince. If I could only elope and take the one, I love. But that will make me a coward before my father. Allah will never forgive me. O brother, sadness cripples in my heart to think of it. I feel the pain.

OLDER BROTHER

But why please others and suffer in return. Never give thy heart in exchange for a kingdom. One day, thy regret will come like a poison beneath thy skin and remind thee of thy love lost.

ELIZABETH-POETRY

In a beautiful dance, like two lovers we become. I embraced thee with secrecy we are hidden from the world. In this dance, thy presence rejoices next to mine. I celebrate the music, and thy spirit. Two lovers we become, and it is thee the angel I see. Purity thou are in my eyes. For I see nay thy past, nor thy evil. I see an angel of light. For I have never seeing an angle's light as the one coming from thy heart. Thus, thy past I have erased with my love, my heart and my life. I completely give my heart to thee. I will die for thee my prince of heart. For my love for thee I cherish with my life. For thee, my beloved I will die, my prince of hearts. I will give my life for thee.

THE PRINCE

Why, why doth love cometh to me now. Why now!
For I have waited for a very long time to feel this
feelings unknown to me. Thy love for me old woman
splashes itself before me like water from the ocean
against the rocks. My unfaithful heart has betrayed
me. And now, my father's demands leave me puzzling
and wondering if I shall leave the kingdom and follow
my heart. O God, why now? Why now? O Allah
forgive me, for my heart aches and my love for her I
cannot hide. Have mercy upon me. Bring peace upon
me, my God. (**He is crying in desperation).**

ENTER THE PRINCE FATHER

I have planned to bring the best food and best band
imported from England chattering company, for thee
and thy princess.

THE PRINCE

Father, such topic of conversation is not my favorite
now. May I please have some time to myself? I beg of
you, father.

FATHER

Is something the matter my son? Is the wedding
stressing thy nerves?

THE PRINCE

Perhaps we can talk another time father. Please, Leave me be alone for now. (With sad expression on his face, he says).

OLDER BROTHER

Brother, I know that expectations are many from the kingdom. And so are the demands. Seek not perfection but follow thy heart. In the end, life is a mere experience of all the moments we live together with memories in our hearts. Listen to thy heart. Follow thy feelings, for true love comes only once.

THE PRINCE

It will do me justice to crush my heart in two. One half, I will give to my beloved, and the other half to my father's desires. This will end all grief or I could simply die in my sleep tonight. Shall I die, my brother? Shall I die? My grief growth deeper and deeper with time as the day to wed Laura is closer with each second. Thus, I feel the need to scape all. O brother, have pity on me for my despair of a love I cannot bared to lose. How can I love and suffer at the same time.

OLDER BROTHER

Why self -torture my brother, why? All things in matters of the heart have a solution. Just follow thy heart. Thou are a rebel in matters of sports but weaken in matters of love concerns. Thy pleasing nature cannot longer be. For thy confusion comes from thy neglect to express true love. Fight my brother, fight for thy love.

THE PRINCE

What would happen if I choose the old woman? The royals will hate me. I will have to simply elope with her. Leave the kingdom, and regret for the rest of my life that I have betrayed the people I love and the kingdom of the Arab world. They depend on me, all of them.

OLDER BROTHER

Fuck the kingdom. They seek only power in exchange for thy sacrifice. Which one will thou seek? Follow thy heart my brother. Do not live in regret.

ELIZABETH POETRY

My heart cannot longer take the anguish of thy absence as a new lover taketh thy heart from me. I shall leave now and never return. Without thy love I feel death cometh upon me. My loneliness is crippling down and I cannot longer stay in this forsaken place where these walls are closing down on me. America is my place of refuge. India will serve me well. For I have been living in a dream like a Cinderella. This castle is now closed and my shiny shoes, I will leave them behind with all the memories of a broken heart I cannot mend because of thee. Goodbye, my prince of hearts.

THE PRINCE FATHER

Finally, she is living and we can be a happy family as we were before.

YOUNGER SON

Father, she is done nothing to our family but love my brother. Is there a sin in love one, who can create laws in the heart of a lover? Her presence has only change my brother. Thankful shall he feel. They love each other, father can you see it?

FATHER

I will not have this conversation about love from a non-qualify ignorant peasant woman. She is not up to royal standards. Speak not to me about this trash of apparent human nature.

YOUNGER SON

What if, thou had fallen for a woman of her status? What would thou have done, father? Thy words are not of kind nature. Such expressions are of a cold and calculated heart. This is so unlike thee father. Release thy hate for her.

FATHER

As pitiful as it seems, she would have been a mistress not a chosen bride.

YOUNGER SON

Mother would have never approved of such actions from thee, father.

FATHER

There are things about life thou are too young to understand son.

YOUNGER SON

I supposed one of it will be falling for an old peasant woman, wouldn't it.

FATHER

Thy generation understands little about respect and moral values. Mine still values family above all. Nothing gets in the way of what my generation and the elders have created. Nothing! A chosen bride we have. This is the tradition and will forever remain.

YOUNGER SON

I hope thou are not disappointment in the end, father.

FATHER

What exactly are thou aspiring to tell me, son.

YOUNGER BROTHER

What if he refuses to marry Laurent? What then, father?

FATHER

Create no doubt in my mind about his chosen bride, or I will not hesitate to dig beneath the heart of my son and make him do as I say.

ACT VIII-SCENE I

OLDER BROTHER

I challenge thee to a dwell. Come brother, get thy magic sword and let's dwell a match. I will have thy head serve on a diamond platter, the most expensive platter ever!

THE PRINCE

Why challenge me when thou are going to be defeated by. Obvious as it seems, I never lose. Are thou certain, my brother?

OLDER BROTHER

Words are that she left to US, aren't thou aware of the news, brother?

THE PRINCE

Words of her I have not heard for days, but to leave? Why leave so drastically, why? She is only running away from love.

OLDER BROTHER

Nay!

THE PRINCE

I will miss her presence, her words, and all her ideas about life and science. Such a great notion of different creations she is. Let's party, my brother.

OLDER BROTHER

No, the dwell is on. I will not let thee drawn in pain, alcohol or sadness. I am here to hold thee, if needed.

THE PRINCE

I cannot go through this, my brother, I can't.

OLDER BROTHER

Never have I seen thee act this way. What exactly is the solution? Tell me brother. Here, grab my sword. I will use this new father bought for me.

THE PRINCE

I can elope, or simply marry the old lady. I feel empty without her. What is it about her that I can't live without? What is it?

OLDER BROTHER

It must be love.

THE PRINCE

Why now, why! A chosen bride is going to be left
behind and hurting from my actions. I am torn to
pieces. I cannot sleep. I think of her, my father and
Laurent. Love is so irrational, so unfair, and so
inexplicable. I never wanted to fall for her, never! I
didn't ask for love. I feel as if I am at war, in a battle
field of my own heart with hers, thus I have never met
her. How can I love her, how? This sounds insane and
irrational to me. I think I have lost my mind.

OLDER BROTHER

Brother I know thou are capable of taking care of this.
Things will come to peace in the end. I trust in thee.
Take this, can thy confused mind compete with me
now. Can it?

THE PRINCE

Go ahead and take advantage of my weakness, my
brother. Never try to compete against a champion. I
have never lost a match. Ever! Never ask for a dwell
unless thou are prepared to lose, my brother.

OLDER BROTHER

We are not done yet!

THE PRINCE

Ego is not enough. One most know how to dwell
in battle. My title was earned through many trials.
Practice, practice my brother, practice.

OLDER BROTHER

Brother, may I confess to thee I am in love with
Amira, my cousin.

THE PRINCE

Amira, why not Laurent, my displeasing anguish will
thou relieve if Laura had been chosen by thee. Blood
relatives are no longer allowed by royal standards.
Amira is our cousin. Bloody hell, what have thou
done, my brother? Wait! Father is calling. I must leave
now. Sorry my brother, this is urgent.

ENTER THE PRINCE FATHER

Yemen is at war. Our presence is being asked upon
by the king. Everybody must be ready by dawn. Our
enemies we shall revenge against and win this war.
A faithful soldier will do anything to win. I expect
nothing but victory not defeat. All my soldiers, I am
with thee and will forever be. I thank thee for keeping
us safe and in peace. May Allah bless all.

ELIZABETH IN AMERICA

My prince, thou are chosen by God, Allah. Thy
heart is fearless against anything. Thy power and
courage have to carry the heaviest of arms across the
sea. Although, thou are always ready to fight for thy
nation; Victory always bring thee to the people of the
Arab world. May Allah be with thee.

SAMEER A SERVANT

Sir, there is a message coming from America. The
prince goes into a rage.

THE PRINCE READING

As magical as it may seem, the goddess travels across
the sea. Then, at times she flies like a bird from place
to place. As a wonderer seeking her spirit where ever
she goes. In vain she looks for a magical moment
when she finally gets it. She knows is I who is sending
the messages, but she recognizes not my silence voice
of love. Endlessly, she tries to understand only to fall
in deep sadness once again.

ELIZABETH

She leans forward with her hands on her cheeks as
she thinks of him. Then a new message on Facebook
arrives.

MESSAGE (V.O.)

If thou are a miracle, my princess, show thyself
to me now. Come to me into my presence. I have
been waiting for thee all of my life. Look into my
soul and tell me that thy love for me has ended. Tell
me. Tell me, my princess. I long to touch thy skin
with gentleness and feel thy angel light next to me.
Perhaps, it is the end of mine. Where are thou my
beloved? Where are thou! I feel death coming upon
me once again.

ELIZABETH

I know of thy war against thy enemy. Please wish
death not upon thy enemy. For to command death
is but to serve it upon thyself. To take a life even by
thoughts is to have no mercy on to thy brother. To kill
is injustice, but to live is a merit for all existence. To
wish death is to serve thy own execution. To love thy
brother is to trust thyself, but to trust thy heart for
killing is not of thy nature. Life is to be preserve not
destroyed. Only that which is true will reveal itself
from within. Love all, but trust only a few. Thy status
is of envy to thy enemy but no one can take who
thou are, no one. War nor hate will ever dissipate thy
enemy. This will only bring them closer to a battle
with thy faith. Love indeed is the cure for such a
pestilence like thy enemy. For only love can turn thy
enemies away with time.

ELIZABETH CONNECTING WITH THE SPIRIT TWIN

Where are thou! I feel death coming upon me once again. Thy soul is not of this world. Is it thee! The twin brother? Thou hath taken thy brother spirit to still his love from him, and thus possess my soul with thy spiritual power. Be in peace. For paradise is glory and earth is not. I have known thy presence is not of this world yet, I recognize not the distinction between both souls. Who are thou my prince of hearts who seek for me with desperation? Thy soul hath possess me like an angel guarding its spiritual gifts from the cosmos above. Who are thou, my prince of hearts? Who are thou?

THE PRINCE- (THE BATTLEFIELD)

I am saying a final goodbye to this bastard. Take his head and send it to the king of hell! War they proclaim against us and war they got. Taketh his head, now!

ELIZABETH-ON FACEBOOK

ELIZABETH- V. O.

Resentment in thy heart is like sending thy soul into a fire of inferno destine by thy thoughts of rage. Leave the grotesque actions to the angels or devils facing their soul. Thoughts of thee have sent him into darkness and light abide not in thee. Say goodbye in peace. Say a final goodbye in peace. If not, thy bloody hands will not be clean by the ocean nor will the color of the sea turn green in hope that thy innocence from sin can be wiped out. Or else, the sea will turn into a rage against thee. Thy sins my prince, will neither be erased by the vastness, power or energy of the sea of forgiveness. Take thy filthy hands and run for hope. Perhaps the air and the creatures of the earth will teach thee kindness, love and wiped out the hate from thy heart. Then, perhaps, thy bloody hands may return to be clean.

THE PRINCE

Why doth she torments me with her words of kindness and parables. Why love cometh to me from a heart I do not know. In the past, love came and went. But now, it remains. Why a peasant woman. Why her, my beloved Allah! Why!

A WEEK LATER-ENTERS THE PRINCE FATHER

My head I hold up high with pried my son. Thy courage hath done our country proud. Revenge is the way to the enemy. I am proud of thee so proud, my son. What words of whispers do I hear about thy decision to marry Laurent? Have I not chosen well for thee, my son?

THE PRINCE

Tell me father, why doth thou divorce mother and married a younger wife? Was it love? Tell me father, can we fight love like soldiers in a battlefield, can we?

101

FATHER

Yes, in matters of the heart no one rules. But thy love cannot attest for any other love but Laurent. It has been done! It is our tradition; it is as old as our grandparents and great grandparents. This cannot be broken. Sorry son.

THE PRINCE

How can thy eyes be so blind father! How?

FATHER

Blind? Has thy desire to persued that woman not been satisfied yet, my son.

THE PRINCE

Father, o father, to know of love is to hear the voice of our god inside of us, for that is what he is, love. Today, he speaks to me in my heart. My heart no longer belongs to me. Place no judgements upon me. My love is not blind, for I can hear the sound of my heart speak words I never understood before. Forgive me father, forgive me.

THE PRINCE FATHER

Thou are in love with that ragged old woman. Impossible! How now? What would I tell Laurent? How will I tell her thy love for her is not more? How! A moment to breathe will serve me well now.

Excuse my presence for I cannot seem to fadden such insolence before me. I can't breathe.

THE PRINCE

Please father, do not make my life an eternal hell. Thou of all the people in this kingdom know very well what is like to love a woman. Why did thou divorce mother? Why? Tell me, why? Thy reasons are not any more Candice than mine. For the first time in my life I feel love for a woman and thou are depriving me the right to love her.

ENTERS THE PRINCE MOTHER

My son, follow thy heart, not thy ego. For love is the basis of what keep us alive. Fill thy heart with this love and fly free as a bird doth in the skies. Set thy spirit free. Be not a prisoner of thy own love. When my heart was left empty, I found refuge in the love of my children. I had something to love. Love the one thy heart calls upon. Go my beloved son, go!

ELIZABETH IN TURKEY

Lovely day by the sun, isn't it? The only thing missing is thee my prince of hearts.

THE PRINCE

Where are thou, can we meet? Can we talk?

ELIZABETH

Call me at my room # 537.

Where are thou my prince, where are thou. Two hours have gone by. No words.

NEXT DAY AIRPLANE

Don't get in the plane, don't! Come with me. He never shows up.

ELIZABETH

Why my prince, why, (Crying uncontrollably). I see happiness through thy eyes, yet thou are about to marry a woman of thy choice. Why hurt me. Revenge thou seek against me for not apparent reason. For only one of evil nature can think of revenge. Doth thy soul rest in the ugliness of nature? I miss thee again, once again I could not find thee. How can a man of noble statute ever think of revenge? Have thou forgotten what mystical power I possess? Why revenge, when all I have for thee is love? My worthiness thou refuse to recognize. Thus, in my heart, only love abides. If I shall never again see thee, my prince, my love for thee will never die nor my heart be empty. I have once again been defeated by thy absence. Where are thou?

FACEBOOK PHOTOS-ELIZABETH

Thou, a miserable bastard! Show thy face to me now! or I will crush your heart with this sword. Turn around and show thy face to me. Now! Thou coward, insipid idiot! Thou have used the prince's photos to deceive me. Why? What reasons thou possess? May Allah forgive thee for thy actions against me, I know who thou are. To love thee is to suffer an eternal life in hell.

ELIZABETH V.O.

O how stupid of me to have fallen for such a trap. How innocent have I been? My heart aches at the thought of knowing that he has used me like an old peace of rag from a dirty bundled of laundry. I must leave Dubai now and never, ever return. (**She cries for hours uncontrollably**). Oh God, what have I done to deserve such actions from a stranger, a man I love for no reason at all? How much hate abides in the heart of one who considers himself to be a brother, a Muslim brother! I have fallen for the wrong man. Have I? My heart does not lie to me. I know that it is thee whom I love. Yet, I have fallen for thee, my Indian man. I love thee my prince, I love thee…

TECHNICIAN

It is all done my brother, all done. Her computer is now clean. She cannot longer have the files or all the ideas she shares with us here in the Middle East. They have been erased. Done!

ELIZABETH

My files, my files, they are all gone! All gone! How can this be, how?

SCENE ACT VIIII SCENE I - ELIZABETH

Could it be, him, the Indian actor, or perhaps, perhaps it is my prince of hearts. Nay, that's not possible, in Paris? I hear the sound of his fancy car. Is it thee my prince of hearts, is it? My heart aches at the thought of knowing that I have once again missed thee. Will I ever meet thee my Prince, will I ever? O Lord, have I been punished for wrong doing or is thy love teaching me how to love a man without a sight of his image. Speak to me, my lord, speak to me. Without him, I feel as if death has come upon me. I cannot leave without his love, or his soul next to mine. He is my inspiration. I live for him, my lord. Please, punish me not for loving him, punished me not lord. For death I will prefer than not to love him. Give me death, lord, give me death. I take thy punishment with death. My heart no longer pulses without his next to mine. He is my life, my love and my soul. Why him, my father, why him! (SHE DIES. THEN, A VISION OF HIM APPEARS BY HER DEATH SIDE).

LAURENT

Die old hag, die! Drink this poison and die. Now I can have my prince to myself. Goodbye! Old hag.

THE PRINCE - V. O.

If love thou denied to me, then my heart I will fill with the last breath of a final goodbye. Resentment in my heart is like poison in my blood. Kiss me one last time before my soul departs. Thy presence will remain with me, not matter where I go. With thee is where my heart belongs. Don't die my beloved, don't die, my lady. Kiss me to say a final goodbye.

ELIZABETH

Taketh me in thy arms one last time and tell me that thy love me. My prince, tell me, tell me my prince before I say goodbye, is there love left for me in thy heart, is there?

THE PRINCE-HOURS LATER

Please, please, I need to know what of her. My soul tells me that she is no longer here with me. I feel her presence living me. I sense everything about her. Tell me that she is still here. Tell me she hasn't departed from this life. Please Ameer, tell me.

AMEER

No breathing, no breathing my prince. I think she has left us. Life is not in her. Her body is cold and fragile. My prince, her soul has departed. She has left us.

THE PRINCE

No… no…why leave now? I have waited this long to meet thee, yet thy presence scape from me like a breeze of the sea so abruptly. Why now my lady, my love. Please Allah, return her soul to me. Please God!!!

AMEER

She has left us, my prince. She is not responding.

THE PRINCE

I will not give up. I know Allah can make any miracle happen. I know. Who could have done this to her. Who?

AMEER

My beloved prince, I know thy faith is strong. But Allah has decided to bring her into paradise.

THE PRINCE

My heart is crushed. For once in my life I love a woman, and now she is gone, gone... Ameer! Ameer! I feel her breathing. She is breathing. Allah has returned her back to me. Allah!!! Shukran! Shukran! Die not my beloved for I have come to thy rescued. Fear not for my love is with thee forever. My wish has been granted by the highest, the only God I know, Allah! He whispers in her ears. Let's elope. Let's go away to a faraway place where no one knows of us. Come, I dare thee to come with me.

ELIZABETH

My prince of hearts thou are. A final goodbye I pledge to thee. Hath death happen to bring this miraculous act of love to me?

THE PRINCE

Run away with me. Let's go far away where no one knows of our presence. Let's elope. Come with me. Come with me, my beloved.

ELIZABETH

My beloved, I have waited this long for God to speak to me, and finally, He has spoken words of love. I have found love at last indeed.

THE PRINCE

Love is all we need. I give my love to thee. Come with me my lady, I will leave it all for thee.

ELIZABETH

Prince of hearts I can see the light in thee. I knew that love will cometh to me one day. I knew God will answer me. He always does. Thy master of love is who I am. I came to teach thee of love and to love thee unconditionally, my beloved prince. Hath death happened to bring this miraculous act of love to me? Thy soul is intertwine with mine, my prince of hearts. Thus, two become one and my love is been share with two souls. I will give my love to thee my beloved, for to love him is to love thee as well. My love is unconditionally spread like the stars across the universe. I see the light in thee as I see in him. Be in peace my beloved. Be in peace.

THE PRINCE

Please, tell me that my love thy will accept, I am here for thee. Tell me. He is crying).

ELIZABETH

For I have come to thee to mend love in thy heart and in thy life. I am the mistress of love which Candice words thy heart will received and treasure forever. Solitude is life without love. Now, my prince, thy heart is filled with love. Share and give what God has given thee.

THE PRINCE

Most faithful I am to my God. If only thee will share thy love with me, my lady. My honor is at stake. Restore my heart and leave with me at once.

ELIZABETH

Nay…my dearest prince. I intend no to tarnish or disrupt the honor of thy royal family. I accept that I am not wanted nor accepted as a woman of honor to have thee, my prince of hearts.

THE PRINCE

Place no hope in my heart for the future. Thou are my future. Reject me not my love, my lady. I can't go on without thy love. Please depart not from my life.

ELIZABETH

Let my love be not a perpetual torture to thy heart.
I am but an old woman as thou refer to me. My love
would last forever. I love thee and I am an old lady.
Go in peace and love.

THE PRINCE

To return without thee, it will be a dishonor to my
pride, my family. I have rather face death. Please!
No… my lady, no! (He is crying and falling to the
ground). **She disappears.**

LADY KATHERINA

Nay, the prince of hearts crying, how could it be? Thy
love for her doth thy denied all this year, and for what
my dearest prince. My expectations of thy strength
are not of a man crying like a child. What has become
of thee my prince?

THE PRINCE

Please leave now. This is not the time.

LADY KATHERINA

If thou want pity, then thou are low. And that is what
I see in this moment of thee, my prince. Let go off
me. Thy hands are forced upon my throat. Why such
despicable behavior, why now. Let go, prince of hell.

THE PRINCE

Lady Katherina, thou have conjured against me with
Laurent. Why? I have loved thee unconditionally all
these years, but nay satisfy thou are not of my love.
Blood is what thou are after. Isn't it lady Katherina?
(To the ground he falls).

THE PRINCE-CONTINUE

Lady Katherina, I can't breathe. I can't breathe! What
actions of hate have thou act upon? I have nothing
but love for thee. Why the hate. I will do anything for
thee. I can't breathe, I can't breathe.

LADY KATHERINA

Since when doth love live in thy heart for her, since
when?, is this one more poetic blasphemy from
thy heart to an old rag, which is neither of appeal
nor status like thee. She gets close to his ears and
whispers. "Who is she to thee my beloved", Take this
and love her forever now. Say it before thy last breath.
Say it! "Who is she to thee"?

OLDER BROTHER

Move away from him! Unfaithful bitch! Go and find
thy place at home. Thy selfish ways have caused
damage to the royals. Thou are the most selfish

woman of evil nature. Leave at once before mother
sees thee. Go! (He cries for help). Help! Help, call an
ambulance. Help! Help! Help, our prince is dying; he
is being stabbed. Help!

ACT X- LAST SCENE

THE PRINCE FATHER

Take her in. She was the last one to be seen with him. I am ordering thee to take her into custody. Now.

OLDER BROTHER

Nay... father big mistake. She is innocent. She wasn't with him when I found my brother. It wasn't her. I cannot disclose such ugly actions.

FATHER

Who then? Speak to me! Speak to me!

OLDER BROTHER

It will destroy our family. Forgive me father, forgive me. I can't disclose the ugly actions against my brother. It will destroy the family.

FATHER

Somebody has to pay, and it may as well be here. She has no one in this land. Who will proclaim her, lock her in!

MOTHER

Thou my beloved, are making a big mistake.

FATHER

Women have no voice in this matter. It is my son's life at stake here. Leave now! Thy presence is not necessary. I have made my decision.

MOTHER

To lock her for life will do no justice. Thou know thy son very well. He will find a way to get her out. May Allah have mercy upon thee! (She bows before him and leaves).

ONE AND HALF YEAR LATER-THE PRINCE BROTHER

My heart aches to know thy suffering my lady. I would have given anything not to have thee suffer in this wall for so long. I know thou have been hiding in fear of being accused on wrong doing. But fear not, my lady, I know the truth.

ELIZABETH

Tell me my beloved, did he marry her, the young lad. Did he? I am now an older woman living in a cocoon of my own yet love has not left my heart. It matters not that I have been away for so long. It matters not for I would have given my heart for his. (She weeps before him).

THE PRINCE BROTHER

Come with me my lady for I know thou had seen it all, felt pain and even death for him. But now, today I come to tell thee the news, the news of him. The prince has died in a hospital in England. Yes, the Prince of Hearts is dead. He died of a heart attack before reaching the hospital. We, in the Arab world mourn his death. We will miss him dearly. He holds her by the hand and say: "Come with me."

ELIZABETH

(in Surprise, she asked) Is that him? The man I communicate with at a distance? Then she exclaimed, "My spooky reaction at a distance has come true." I have waited all my life to meet this interesting man of mystic nature. The inventor of the future. Suddenly she faints. The prince brother leaves silently and she remain with her mystical dream man. Her dream finally comes true. The man lifts her off the ground and carries her away.

Then her dream comes true.

Cut!

About The Author

Frances Mahan is an author, screenwriter, public speaker, and strategic intervention coach who enjoys science and technology. She writes poetry in Shakespearean style and loves to travel, read, and appreciate nature.

Printed in the United States
By Bookmasters